James Hook
1746–1827

Easy Duets

Leichte Duette

for Descant and Treble Recorder
für Sopran- und Altblockflöte

Edited by / Herausgegeben von
Hans Magolt

ED 8878
ISMN 979-0-001-12370-9

SCHOTT

Mainz · London · Berlin · Madrid · New York · Paris · Prague · Tokyo · Toronto

© 2000 SCHOTT MUSIC GmbH & Co. KG, Mainz · Printed in Germany

Inhalt

Preface

James Hook, the son of a cutler, was born in Norwich in 1746 and died in 1827 in Boulogne. Although born with crippled feet, he was enabled to walk with a limp by means of early operations. He was regarded as a *Wunderkind*, playing the harpsichord at the age of four and performing in public from the age of six.

Following the early death of his father – James was only 11 years old at the time – he had to earn his own living by giving concert performances and instrumental tuition for guitar, piano, violin and German flute. In 1763/64 he settled in London where he was successful as an organist, not only in churches but also in Vauxhall, the most famous of London's pleasure gardens..

James Hook was one of the leading musicians of London society. He specialized in composing light entertainment music. He wrote the most diverse works for pleasure gardens, but also many organ concertos, an oratorio, several stage works and operas, over 2000 songs and countless teaching pieces for various settings.

The easy duets for descant and treble recorders presented in this volume originate, in part, from the 12 Duettinos Op. 42, the other pieces are occasional works without opus numbers.

Vorwort

James Hook wurde als Sohn eines Messerschmiedes 1746 in Norwich geboren und starb 1827 in Boulogne. Obwohl er mit verkrüppelten Füßen auf die Welt gekommen war, konnte er sich dank mehrerer früher Operationen hinkend fortbewegen. Er galt als Wunderkind, das bereits mit vier Jahren Cembalo spielte und mit sechs Jahren öffentliche Konzerte gab.

Nach dem frühen Tod seines Vaters – James war gerade einmal elf Jahre alt – musste er sich seinen Lebensunterhalt durch Auftritte in Konzerten sowie als Instrumentallehrer für Gitarre, Klavier, Violine und Flöte verdienen. 1763/64 ließ er sich in London nieder, wo er als erfolgreicher Organist tätig war, allerdings nicht nur in Kirchen, sondern auch in Vauxhall, dem berühmtesten aller Londoner Vergnügungsparks.

James Hook gehörte zu den führenden Musikern des Londoner Gesellschaftslebens. Bei seinen Kompositionen bildete die leichtere Musik einen seiner Schwerpunkte. Er schrieb die verschiedensten Werke für Vergnügungsparks, außerdem aber auch zahlreiche Orgelkonzerte, ein Oratorium, mehrere Singspiele und Opern, über 2.000 Lieder und unzählige Unterrichtsstücke für verschiedene Besetzungen.

Die in diesem Band enthaltenen leichten Duette für Sopran- und Altblockflöte entstammen teilweise den 12 Duettinos op. 42, teilweise sind es Gelegenheitswerke ohne Opuszahl.

Minuet

Edited by / Herausgegeben von
Hans Magolt

James Hook
1746-1827

Descant Recorder
Sopran-Blockflöte

Treble Recorder
Alt-Blockflöte

49 304

Gavotte I

Gavotte II

Gavotte III

Vivace

Andantino

rit.

Fine

D. C. al Fine

Tempo di Minuetto

Allegretto

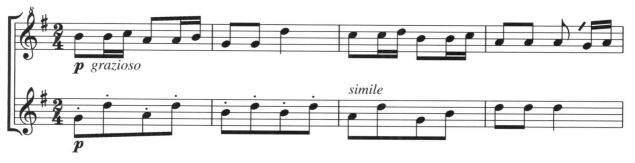

Allegro ma non troppo

Allegro
(in Kanonform)

Rondo

Fine

rit.

D. C. al Fine

Duettino I

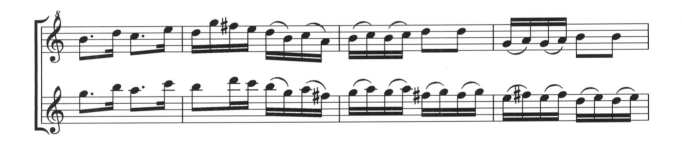

Minuetto

This page is left blank to save an unnecessary page turn.
Aus wendetechnischen Gründen bleibt diese Seite frei.

Rondo

Allegro con spirito

Fine

D. C. al ⊕ - ⊕

D. C. al Fine
(A-B-A-C-A)

Duettino II

Allegro

Fine

Minore

D. C. al Fine

March

Duettino III

Minuetto cromatico

Schott Music, Mainz 49 304